MW01595076

LOVING WITH EMOTIONS

You Must Feel Everything

Keshia L. Williams

Kindle Direct Printing 2020

In Loving Memory of my Mother Simett Williams,
may you continue to Rest Peacefully.

CONTENTS

INTRODUCTION

I hope you may recongize the process, and the raw emotions expressed in this journey called life. I titled this masterpiece Loving with Emotions because of the ordeals we my encounter, or know of someone who has told you a excerpt of their life experiences.

Pleases enjoy and feel every emotion.

12 O'CLOCK

I know you don't want to talk to me, and I know I said shit I can't take back, and I won't... But it seems like us being friends will always be distant. I love you and it doesn't change and I wish sometimes I never met you and I wouldn't feel this way. I say how I feel, and I know if you said it first it'll be so much harsher. But you don't love me the same way I love you and it makes it so much harder.

A HEART

A Heart deserves an even better one to show them that life isn't always about give and take. Life is also about reciprocation. Love is similar when accepting what you cannot change but turning it into something beautiful if you are willing to go the extra mile. Love and Life are neck and neck because the same thing you are trying to build can be destroyed in selfish acts. I had a conversation the other day about relationships, and I brought that up to say we weren't put on this Earth to be alone. Find that Self Love, find that Self Time to know what you want and what you don't want. Do Not Allow a Temporary situation ruin what could be memories to cherish.

A PLACE

I'm going to take you to a place
A place you may not want to stay
A place where you will cry
A place where things aren't okay
That place is my heart
It's cracked in the middle
It's stabbed from behind
the front and both sides

After I will take you to my Soul
It's deep and kind a creepy
But it has its solitude
Where our worlds can collide
And some of me you will be consuming
But that's a short trip

Lastly, I'll let you invade my Mind
The one place I don't allow anyone to touch
Where my private thoughts are
The place that allows all this to work
My prize possession and my one true sacred place
Where people think they can read you and they don't know much
or don't know how to face
Face what's a false reality and what's Actually real
I'm taking you to a place, to learn how to feel.

BRIEF THOUGHTS

A hurting heart is fragile, but we all bleed the same blood.
No one knows your pain better than you or who does?
I want to cry sometimes but my pride won't let me.
My doubts, my conscious, my trust, my loyalty...
I think sometimes why can't I find a guy to spoil me.

I've been great,
I've been awesome, shit perfect as can be, but alone I still remain.
And I pray one day I'll meet he.

CHANGE

Do yourself a favor... Stop trying to change the one you're with
You met them and you liked them for who they were
So, check your perimeter because maybe there's something about
Yourself you don't like
We can only control ourselves and nothing else
If they've done something that has caused you discomfort
That's when lines of communication need to be encountered
Not vindictive or violent acts
Not petty shenanigans or cheating
Talk to the one you love because love isn't supposed to hurt
It's about acceptance and united healing

CLARITY

She ran away to see the day
She could breathe and get some control
She wanted to fix all the things she did wrong
She felt like she was the problem
She didn't know what to do
She seeks comfort in trying to mend broken hearts too
She wasn't a preacher, a psychologist, but a helper
She felt she had a gift, a purpose to serve
She once was a victim, a murderer, a person of choice words
She was an optimistic, at times negative, and sometimes cynical
She looked at things in all prospective, but always wanted things residue
She wasn't perfect, not the greatest, but did everything to the best of her ability
Because the world outside her window gave her the perfect opportunity.

AWARENESS

I have a lot of women to thank today
Yet through the birth my heart broke first
She said she'd be there for me, but I was there for her
I broke all the rules, stood up, no longer a little girl
As a pawn I only knew what was next to come
Then later the young lady had her a son
The middle child I claim the fame
Just on my license plate
That if I knew back then what I knew now
I always pray to the lord my soul to take
That I always did what was right and I may have done some wrong
But I got on my knees to pray
And I also read my psalms
Ashes to ashes, dust to dust is 23
But I pray at night sometimes please come rescue me
I died 4 times in my life yet I'm still breathing
And yet people be tripping over social media like its appeasing
You put your life on air like it's a paid event
But what you forgot to mention was that dark place you were afraid to take part in
You play on your own thoughts because your likes get you noticed
But what you forgot besides your body, lips, hips
If what else keeps you focused
The Brain is the sexiest thing besides your smile
Besides the S you think you wear on your chest
Got you thinking out loud
How much of your body will you sale

Before you stop breathing
Is social media just your outlet on life
Or the only reason you're still existing...

COMPLIMENTS

How is it that I hold my head up high
And yet I feel unwanted
Unwanted by the man who claims he loves me
But I get my hair done, nails done
And yet it goes unnoticed
Oblivious to my Appearance
But negative slurs are always heightened
Yet I'm never scared to be alone
As for you I think you're frightened
Why hold on to me if there's nothing there
Why share a bed with me if the Glass is half empty
Don't get mad if another Man pay Attention to me
I'm Sexy, I'm Sassy, and yet still in Love
If I go my own way there will be no Sympathy
Just plain Survival of the Fittest
Because while you were down the Street...
After I got my hair done, he was just Staring at ME...

Compliments.

DEALING

I put in a few transfers
No, I didn't share
No longer could I possibly care
Care about what everyone else was doing
All I knew is that I wanted to get out
And get away from the pain
From all the people and things driving me insane
From all the Favors and Borrowing
From not being paid back or the occasional calling
From all the time I came through in the clutch
How often I thought if I disappeared...
Who actually loved me that much
To see if I was missing...
If I was under a rock
If my heart was beating...
Or if I was left for dead or shot
But no one called.
So, I learned how to cope...
That even without the bad dope
The alcohol and the users
Dealing was something that I was use to
I had to break out the norm And Focus on me
I HAD TO MOVE ON FROM JUST EXISTING

DEPARTURE

He no longer wanted to be selfish
He left her a long time ago...
But he kept her close enough to let her know
He couldn't do this anymore
He chose to stay just a little longer for her to believe
That all he was doing was for them
But all he was doing was slowly packing to leave
He pretended that everything was ok
He even tried sleeping on the couch to make it make sense
But a pillow she cried in and his presence didn't help
She felt like her world was snatched away
She broke down every so often
And at times he'd wipe her tears away
But she couldn't believe the hand she was dealt
All she did was allow herself to open up
She wanted to be loved and share her bed again
She had just walked away from years of hurt
And what she thought was going to be marriage
She was determined to make a way
She had a plan to try to get him to stay
She brought him a ring
But he said he didn't want to hurt her, and he went on his way.

DISAPPEAR

You can't be the only one trying to make a situation work...
But if your effort goes Unnoticed...
Make it A Point to Disappear.

DOUBT

I thought when we met
We would hit it off
And yet another disaster
I thought when I gave you me
It would have a reaction
But you reacted with dissatisfaction
Like I didn't matter
I allowed you to take my thoughts
And turn them to controversy
That I thought I mattered to you
Because you damn sure mattered to me
But, yet again another failure
Yet I still forgave you
Without a shadow of a doubt
You were nothing but another stranger.

DREAMS

He appeared like a thief in the night
She wondered where he came from
He put his finger across her lips
He said," Do not be afraid Love"
I'm here to protect you
Please do not fear me, I am here
She became frightened, closed her eyes...
He later disappeared
She had awakened the next day in such dismay
But gotten up and started her way
She remembered he was handsome, tall, and baritone
She knew it was just a dream and shook it off
She went outside, and went to work
She crossed the street and there he stood
He walked up to her and then he said...
Good morning my love, I want to hold your Hand.

DUI

I Didn't know loving you so much
Would one day backfire on me
I got arrested because of a technicality
I tried to figure out if you ever cared for me
Or for you was it Humility
I think you had gotten joy out of seeing me in a bad situation
But when you need me
It was then to your Obligation
That I thought I meant more to you
Each and every time I felt used
I kept saying I was going to leave and wasn't coming back
But you'd say you needed me and again I believed it
Then when you left again
I'd be heated
Continuously abusing my mental capacity
That giving you the benefit of the doubt no longer satisfied me
That I had an addiction
You were my BAD DOPE
Every time I'd say NO
I'd go back for more
Every time I took a hit
It left me Yearning
I tried to resist but it grabbed me
The hold it had was so Everlasting
It was hard to stay away...
But Ever so Later I had gone without my FIX
That I knew I'd Miss
But I had to move on from this BAD HABIT.

FOOD FOR THOUGHT

People that come into your life for a reason
Sometimes not just for a season but
Never underestimate something you need
For something you want...

FORGIVENESS

I said I was sorry
I had apologized
I said I wouldn't do it again
But you continue to undermine me
You continue to Lie
You tell me you aren't doing this or that
But I find out in the oddest way
You get upset, even angry
But yet you are the one in the wrong
And I keep holding on
I keep my balance
I remain strong
Then I had to take a minute
I had to recover
That I Forgave you for me
But what was it worth
Did you deserve it
I need a moment in my own peace
I had to remember I never needed you
You needed me

FRIEND

Love and light
She was my friend
Just like my sister
She took something I said
And it missed her
I thought she was like me
and I let her in
But she disregarded me
Like some of her men
I walked by faith and not by sight
But I don't do emotions
And I walk away being polite.

FROM ME TO YOU

The day I met you I wasn't looking for anything
The day I seen your smile it uplifted me
Our conversation was comforting
Your eyes lit me up
Your voice was soothing
Your brain ignited something inside me
That he may be a gift
Friendship is awesome
And getting to know you is a prize
I hope you get your prize of your journey
That the mirror you look in enlightens your integrity
That I know you are strong, your strength brings infamy
To be the greatest you, you can be.

GENERAL THOUGHTS

You can never live your life in the past and must move forward to greener pastures... You will endeavor hardships. Any part of a crystal stare wasn't counted on. But if you allow something that seems real in your life, you are the one that has created these overly capsized delusions. The truth was always in front of you, you just wish not to see because people tend to reform to fit someone else's view or identity. In which that means they only have done what you expected them to do. All this time their TRUE self was bound to show up. People as we know are creatures of habit. There is also the do unto other as you want done unto you.

Life's lessons are moments to remember, you will move on to bigger and better things. It's ok at times to be vulnerable just don't be knave. It's ok to hug someone, or just do things you're not use to because you can make each other become fulfilled.

It's funny how some people give there all to the undeserving, but somehow entertain and embellish on nothing. The love and care of the opposing can be turned away when they have caused no pain at all. I've known hurt and it'll only last as, long as you want it too. Don't be afraid to feel for someone else that has always been there no matter what. Love is an action channeled through your emotions, through someone's presence or absence, there touch can always become so much more once you let it...

.

GIFTS

At 7 years old I had a gift
To write books or be a normal child and play
My mom said be a kid baby
But I grew up way too fast
I occupied my time with clubs, and music
Yet there was something I lacked
I was aggressive and I was smart
Which brought me to this conclusion
Do something you love and I'm finally putting it on paper
It's not just how you live your life
But how you leave a stain
And there's nothing else to prove
It's not about how you claim the fame
It's what you do with it
Just keep calm and be present
It's not only how You lived your life
it's about
What you do with it.

HEARTS

Our hearts have been broken
Sometimes in two
But eventually I'll stop being in love with you
No matter the hurt, no matter the pain,
It's something that has misplaced me

In a drought, turned inside out with some undecided anger
But further inspection to my recollection
You tried to make a fool of me.

Hell, hath no fury for a woman scorn
My thoughts bewildered me
someday I know you will remember me
I pray God takes away my pain in such
Hopefully sooner than later

I'll watch what I do with my heart and can stay awhile longer
No more hoping and dreaming
Soon one day I shall know
If he wants, She

I'll never have to play games or Run
Run away from his grasp because he'd never let go of me
His prize possession, his love, and his One and only
No more searching because I no longer want to seek to find
If he's looking for me
It'll happen in a matter of Time...

HUMBLE

Don't be so Quick to Brag about what you Got.
It can easily turn into what you Had...
Humble yourself...

I MISS

I MISS the Comfort
I MISS the UPs and DOWNs
I MISS the Random Movie Nights...

I MISS LOVE

I REMEMBER

I remember when there was pen to a paper
Now it's fingers to text
How do you express your love
If I can't look in your face
There aren't emotions behind fingers
There're only unjust words
How if I read it on paper, I knew what it was
It was more heart felt, it really felt deep
That you would pour out your feelings on paper for me
Now emojis take precedence
And you say it was what I meant to say
But auto correct has taken the place
Taken the place of many actions we lock away
It'll keep you from saying the things you meant to say
Just like having a baby can only keep him with you in time
That I wish I could take it back before the Internet took over our
lives.

THOUGHT

I Thought I needed you
But I didn't
I put my pants on the same way
You do
I button my shirt like
You do
But no tie
Unless I want to flex
Different is necessary
My gender is a difference
But my sex is the message
I changed your life in some way
And with me you learned some thing

I

I stayed by you
I've held your hand
I was demanding and understanding
I was strong and persistent
I applied my best interpersonal skills
I used my leverage, I was untouchable
Because my honesty is everything, I hold dear
I wish 9 years ago....
My heart wasn't so open

IN LIFE

In life I gave so much
My heart I gave so much trust
I dug so deep to find what was inside of me
That I died trying to remind me
Of what was to not be who I Should be
To change, so people would like me
To put my pride to the side to hold on
Hold on to the same enemies that dislike me
To break bread to fit in
When I always stood Out
Then I had to realize the same people, that told me to change had
so much envy
That all this time I wasn't pretending
But you were scared of me

INTRODUCTION

I know a lot of people
I have yet to be phony
Unless that comes from a person that doesn't really know me
I'm guarded and reserved
But you may hear different
You are entitled to your difference of opinion
I'll give it to you straight, I'm real and can be misinterpreted
But you could never walk a day in my shoes
My 7 1/2 you can't wear it
My future is bright, and it remains to be seen
Hi, my name is Keshia, nice to meet you
And now you know my name

IS THERE

Is there genuine love
Is there sincerity left

Can we share everlasting moments
Or live in painful neglect

That we gave each other a promise
And we break them every time
He called you a BITCH
Or you called him a Motherfucking Lie

Where did it all go

What happened to our Loyalty, Honesty, and Peace...

That when we stared into each other's eyes...
We'd give one another what we need...

That I breath you in and I exhale all the unnecessary
That even though you piss me off
I'll be here to carry
Carry all the burdens we are supposed to fight...
Together
That I say all these things with the intentions to hurt you...
Never

JUDGEMENT

You chose to read it
You chose to open this book
31 years on this planet and look how long it took
I'm an open book
But you still try to judge me
But the raw and uncut edition
But through these years I still get down on this mission
To become a better, me
I serve my God, the position he leads me to become a protege
I love myself it took 21 years to find it
But I appreciate the time to accept it
Don't misunderstand the conception
It takes time to perfect it
My eyes are brown, my skin is kind of light
But it takes a real woman to love her flaws
I could care less about a hater in site
I don't burn bridges but if I do, I'm through
The many challenges of life will do that to you
I'm a sinner not a saint, but I repent
Judge not to be judge first
No one knows the demons you are dealing with.

KESH

The heart wants what it does
But decisions have to be made
I put my everything into everybody
But I never get the same
I didn't do it for gifts
I didn't do it for acceptance
That rhythm between my chest
Was all I ever needed
I was supposed to be the Star
Be this great singer
Or be an author
I gave everyone infamous words
I spoke life into believing
To just be yourself and be awesome
I came bearing my soul, I just wanted to give love to those
Those individuals I thought deserved it
I loss my loved ones and I kept the same message
That you do unto others as you want done unto you
People can't understand your pain
They only know what they see
But they say what's understood doesn't need to be explain
I had to finally start worrying about me

LET GO

I leave you, you follow me
I block you, you find a way
You act like you can't be without me
But there was no reason for me to stay
You call me, you email me, when you can't get through
Yet you have the fairy tale and I faced the news
You left me long ago, and you're the one holding on
Please Leave me alone I'm not doing this anymore

LETTER 2

Maybe this wasn't a good idea in the first place because you still treat me like I mean nothing and yet I'm the one left crying or disappointed. You still treat me like I'm nothing. And besides anything else if relative I try to believe you might still care but you don't. I'm just another piece of ass that's expendable to you because If I weren't you wouldn't throw me away as if you didn't tell me you wanted to, spend the night or time with me. Again, my fault trusting or attempting to believe that it was still something there.

LOVE, SEX, LIES, AND DECEIT

I loved you from you Head down to your Feet
I played along half the time
I swore up & down
I knew you were mine
But you weren't solely mine
Then the love slowly turned boring
And I often felt lonely
The coldness seemed just like business
The emotions later started lacking
The love had changed
I No longer had a partner and our relationship wasn't up for claim
That our bond would never be the same
That the game finally changed on me
You said Forever & Eternity
That the whispers in my Ear turned to silent calls
I did not know my love anymore
That the Betrayal I Endeavored was costly
That the thoughts clouded my mine unknowingly
That, that wet pillow was my escape
And yet the sex we use to have
Only reminded me of how this was a mistake
Of how you took my kindness for weakness
How I still cooked & Cleaned
And yet it was meaningless...
That eventually it turned to hate & later bitterness...
Because I stayed too long, fighting an endless battle and my emo-

tions led me on
Because my pride lost the adrenaline to fight for what I knew I
wanted
That every time you said You loved me
Your Lies cut deeper & deeper
I lost a part of my sanity
How could I love someone so much I forgot about the reasons?
How did I break my heart so bad?
That I felt like there was nothing left
With these words I can finally put these feelings to rest
That I gave too many privileges & you made them your rights
Now I'm left to fight these demons inside
I chose you, I trusted you Fully and whole heartedly
But you brought me to my knees
You poisoned me
Death Before Dishonor
I broke my own heart

But just because I lost the battle didn't mean I'll never win the war
The thought of light breaking through my window, or at the end
of the tunnel
The Love within doesn't come from MEN, but through my Pain
and Struggle.

LOVE

Love is not just something you say
Love is something you do
You don't roll out of bed one day in it
Then the next day it's Fuck them
You can be the most unaffectionate person
But we all have emotions
Whether you do it alone, or you just have hidden agendas
Keep in mind everybody needs somebody
Love has no limits, but to some, pain is bliss
Don't stay in a situation if it's not worth it
Learn to deal with things without running out the door.
Things can get complicated and some things can become stagnant
But it's up to you to make your relationship work.
An outsider can always look in
But could never understand what you two share
Loyalty is the hardest thing to subdue, unless you're just a free spirit
Just don't set someone else up because of temptation or infatuation
Everyone needs to understand Mutual respect and compromise
because looking into someone's eyes
and deceiving them is unforgivable.
Love has no limits
No boundaries
No feelings for any reason...

LOYALTY

Not many people are willing to be with A person from the ground up.
They want to skip the blood, sweat, and tears and get straight to the benefits.
If someone is willing to be patient with you, pray for you, encourage you, and
cheer you on to your goals....
You should recognize that and act accordingly.
Appreciate and Respect those who were there from the start.
LOYALTY IS EVERYTHING

MAY 11TH

You know that feeling when the world is on your shoulder's yea
me too
That moment in time when you feel like your world is crashing
Been there too many times
But I guess I'm letting my FAITH waiver
I guess maybe I'm being selfish to not appreciate what's in front of
me
That I have breathe in my body
That I have blood flowing through my veins
That I know pain only last as long as you want it to
And there is sunshine after the rain
That the person staring at me is Strong and Witty
That the one that cries alone knows love and sympathy
That crying it out and talking doesn't make you weak
That no matter the struggle you are facing
Will one day be a distant Memory.

MOTHER

She gives you everything
She loves you with everything
She forgives you no matter the Cost
One day she'll be gone but not Lost
Tell Your Mother You Love Her

MY ALL

I did my best and All I had gotten was a broken heart
Now I can't sleep, of all the things you meant to me
I feel like I can't breathe, please take this pain away from me.

I gave you my all, it wasn't good enough
I gave you my trust, you took this away from us
But now I see you weren't right for me.
Somebody please come take this pain away from me.

Every day I tried, every night I cried
I just wanted to make it work
But you never had plans for me
I constantly fought myself because I was so confused
I don't know what to do. I was so in love with you
It will never be the same
With time there comes change
Now there's nothing left to do but walk away.

I gave you my all, it wasn't good enough
I gave you my trust, you took this away from us
But now I see you weren't right for me.
My love stayed true to you
You hurt me in the worst way
Loving again I don't know if I can do...

MY BEST FRIEND

To my best friend
I love you and you're my sister
we have our differences
I try my best for you to trust me
And I think you disregard those things
I don't need outlandish credit
I sometimes want reassurance
My broken heart looks for gratitude
But my heart gets instant gratification
We've been through some ups and downs
But you are my sister where it counts
I hope we can keep moving forward
And always express to each other what is meant
But through God I know it all makes sense
That we make things work and the time we spend is genuine

OCTOBER 5TH

I don't know if I'm setting myself up
You gave me something to think about
Now you are on my mind constantly
Am I overzealous or just unfocused
Or maybe I was just caught up in the moment
It's been awhile since I've been courted
Hell, I haven't held hands either
It may be too early for reassurance
But I wouldn't take back the short time we've spent neither
Even if it doesn't last
I can appreciate the company
It could be meant to be
Or God sent you to me as a reminder
To remind me of what I am worth
Getting to know you I'm so immersed
Your conversations capture me
And your eyes hypnotize mine
In my mind you seem like a present
Sent from above
You may read this like who says this after two weeks
No really... who does
But I could care less I say what's on my mind
And whatever it maybe
It will happen in Due Time

ON MY MIND

You can spend your whole life trying to make others happy, but you must do what makes you happy. You must start by not blaming yourself for everything that goes wrong. If you made a conscious effort, then that's all that counts. I spent my whole life trying to create happiness for others and it often backfires on me. I try to put myself out there and the same thing occurs. I never really dated and sometimes I don't want to because I end up crying and hurt that I put myself out there. Or I do too much, and I feel like I always must prepare myself for the worse in the beginning.

OPENING UP

I would like to open up together
And it is not one sided
I just don't want to give too much
And Let my pride be hurt again.

PAY ATTENTION

I asked him if he wanted me to cook for him
He said I got it
I asked him if he wanted me to rub his back
He said I'll be alright
I asked could we just cuddle and watch a movie
He said He was busy
I asked him could we go to dinner
He said he wasn't hungry

So, I started going out by myself...

I grabbed lunch and brought home flowers
He asked, "who were you with"
I went to a matinee
He asked did I go alone
I brought home Vickie secrets
He asked who are those for...

But what he didn't see
for once he paid attention to all the things
he only viewed negatively not realizing...

I started loving me

POTENTIAL OF A MAN

I liked his style
I loved his scent
I gave him a hint of swag
I admired his intelligence
He was always in the present
I focused on the future
He was taking care of his priorities
I wanted my empire to be immense
I liked how he maneuvered
I liked how he handled his business
SO, I wanted more and to see what was at Stake
I got what I wanted & more than I bargained for
I realized the risk I'd taken
I fell in love with thoughts of what we could make and have
I fell for what I created...

The Potential of a Man

QUESTIONS

If I was your only
Would you do right
Would you be by my side
Would you hold me down
Make me feel safe
Love me more & more Everyday
Not to cheat, just to explore me
Know every single part of me
Know what not to do to make me trip
Know what makes me happy, and what makes me sad
Know when I need alone time, or be here when I'm upset
Know the difference when I say leave and it really means stay
To know if we have an argument, I love you anyway...

REALIZED

I gave you a home
I gave you my heart
I gave you my trust
I gave you a start
A start over to fix, what was broken in your life
With no limits to hold you back to be free of all strife

I gave you a chance
I gave you a choice
But you left me with no voice
You got what you needed
Then you threw me away
Just like a dog does a bone
When it has lost its taste

I swallowed all I had left but was still angry
You apologized, I let you back in
I forgave he
I met my demise
But it only came naturally
The babies kept coming and there wasn't room for anymore Sorry

RECOLLECTION

We had talked about the plan
We said what would take place
As usual you managed to knock my smile right off my face
You said you were coming
I prepared myself and waited
Again, the time had gotten away from you

Yep that text I'm Reading
Looking in the mirror with great disappointment
I asked myself why and wipe off my make up
I was dressed very pretty, and decided I had enough
Then A following text came through I Love You Very Much
I try not to be Hasty, We Put in so much time
Then it finally hit me, you weren't just Mine.

REMINDERS

You find out the things you need to know when it's over
When they feel like their life is so much better without you
When they can openly speak their fuck ups on the phone
When you were the problem and they weren't
That's when you did everything you could it didn't matter at all
When they're still trying to sleep with you
When they act like they never needed you
They're just playing with you
Just to see how far they could go
When you realized you actually dodged a bullet
And you see things that you've done, but you said you wouldn't
When that confused feeling starts to come into your mind
Of how you gave so many years and you wasted so much time
That I'm glad I was selfish, and I got up and walked away
I'm not the fool walking around while you're out playing around
on me.

ROSE COLORED GLASSES

You have her looking crazy
I guess you think it's cool
But what she doesn't know won't hurt her
But you can only choose to play the fool
It's not my problem, I turn the other cheek
But I don't believe those rose-colored glasses
Fit you perfectly
You aren't having fun, so you chose to settle
Baby he'll never be on your level
I'm sure if he wasn't obligated, he'll forget you
To each is own, blood, sweat, and tears
Sometimes it's better to walk this earth alone
Then to go through all these emotional changes.

SANCTUARY

We all seek it and we try to find it
Some of us had it all along but let it go
It can be deep inside you
Or you can look for it in someone else
You know that place where you are at peace
Where everything is alright, and you have what you need
It gives you solace; you can just get lost in it
It gives you pause; you take a minute to reflect
Where you go to disconnect
It's safe, it's warm from the cold
It doesn't have to be intimacy
We are all here temporarily
But in your Arms, I call it

Sanctuary

SELF-AWARENESS

If you keep providing the Fantasy
You'll never get the Reality you Deserve...

Be your own kind of wonderful
And you'll be treated with Class...

SHE AND HE

She gave good love
He gave her moments
She gave him 8 years
He gave her Bullshit
She gave him Trust
He gifted her with Deceit
She gave him up
He died every time in his Sleep.

SHE

I know how it felt
Because she was me
At one point
Yet I failed to realize

Just LIES... And You Ruined me

WHEN I

When I give it doesn't come with strings. I'm not
keeping track of what I gave you or what you think
you owe me. When I give, I choose to do so without
ulterior motives. I give because I'm genuine. I give
because I know what it's like to be without, to long
for and be ignored, to speak and not be heard, to
care for and get nothing in return. When I give it's
because I understand, and I know the value in what
I have in my heart. I refuse to let the world stop
me from sharing that. But when things start being
taken for granted. When you no longer appreciate
my sincerity. I won't switch up. I won't get angry,
and I won't be spiteful. I'll just get smart and I'll
change your role in my life. Because when I give, I'm
all in. But When I'm done, there's no coming back.

SIGNS

I had sign long time ago
Telling me to leave you alone
But my heart wouldn't let me stray
And the pain kept me in the days
That this is all I have
Never will these things change
But I had to see you for who You were
Knowing things would Never be the same.

SINGLE

Being single isn't the end of the world
It's the just the tip of the iceberg
Once you learn how to get along (by yourself)
You've mastered being human...

WAITING ROOM

If you can care for me
Then loving me shouldn't be so hard
If you reach out for me and I'm not there
Baby I'm never too far
If you choose to walk away remember the touch of my kiss
That the thoughts run through my mind of how you I will miss
You can leave me be and say you feel nothing more
But inside we both know you didn't want to walk out the door...

Being torn between what's right, and wrong tore the situation in 2
Now the days pass by but still somehow, some way I miss you
These are feelings that are suppressed, but somehow show up
from time to time.
That when you're not really seeking love You it will find
I don't want pillow talks and what could be
I want you to show me how it all wasn't a dream
These are things on my mind that I feel like writing
This isn't always a thing of the past, but I wouldn't mind inviting

Never ashamed to say I've been hurt before, and I have put up that
barrier
Because at this point I couldn't be any happier
No stress, No arguing
Just me, myself, and I
If I have to cry, I don't have to sit and wonder why
If he loves or why he does the things he does
Because I have me on my agenda and I punch that clock when I'm
through.

Men make it hard, but some females made it even worse
When you're always available to pick up your skirts
We use to get dates
Now dudes look at us as bedding to be made...

You wonder why he left? It's either 2 reasons he only wanted one thing, or he can't be committed. Or just maybe you didn't bother getting to know the inside just the physique. Now you're mad that he's probably screwing your friend that was already eyeing him when you were just to blind to see. Oh, yea your right hand will take your leftovers trust and believe. Long as she thinks you didn't put it down, she going to give him everything he needs... sorry it's the truth. Chicks can be so scandalous too... that's why I learned my lesson... watch how you move...

SKELETONS

On bending knees praying
That the love we could be making
That you've been with another

Yet I ask myself
do I deserve
Deserve to be naive and misguided
You say I'm trippin' and I know you hide it
That every time I look at you
My true intent is slighted
All the things I want to say
But my love subsides it

Sleepless nights and tired mornings
I lay beside you, but my heart is constantly mourning
That feeling we use to share
That we stay pretending we care
At your smile I use to stare
Now all I feel is much despair
What are we holding on to
Do we even know
I thought we could get through anything
Hell, even grow, Grow passed the pain
Let it all out, let it show
That We never really wanted to be together
We just didn't know how to let go

SOME OF ME

I'm not Always trying to be hard
But being trusting left some Scars
My Loyalty was Honest
But disappointment Eventually Set in
Not Being the Typical Female Set in
But I've been Broken
Even Telling you I liked you...
I felt like I was over stepping
Overstepping my boundaries because you didn't want to let any-
one in
It's hard to not like you
You're Attractive and I Love your company
You just don't know how hard I try not to... push you away from
me.

SOME POINT

They say be optimistic and don't be negative,
but when do you open your eyes to the
         nonsense in front of your face

Recognize the Red Flags in the beginning to not put up
with the same things you've dealt with Before.

SOMEONE ELSE

The craziest thing about life is...
That we've all made somebody better...
For someone else...

SOMETHING TO
THINK ABOUT

They kiss you gently, they hurt you deeply
But you still love hard
They lie, they console you
You see through the scars
You take their hand, you try to understand
See what's more than skin deep
You put trust in them, you give them your heart
You start to eventually lose energy
You keep the faith, Pray for another day
Things seem at peace
Something goes wrong, Feelings no longer strong
Everything Messes with you mentally
Somedays you're mad, Somedays you're sad
Their embrace makes it better
You try again, Hoping then
It'll all be different
She makes you mad, He makes you angry
You scream and bicker
You cry your tears, they wipe your face
As you make love the candle flickers
You taste the sweet flavors, you embrace the thought of Ecstasy
Then you see, You and I make WE
And we still have possibilities
That thru all the pain, it has transitioned
That there's not another minute, you'd rather be missing
Ups and Downs, Falling outs

Can be mended...

That You and I, that is Love, and Every Moment Together We Spent... We Meant IT

ONE PERSON

That one person that makes you feel great
But you can't have them
That one person you wanted just for you
But you made them better for someone else
That person you gave your all
But they stomped on your heart
That person you gave everything to
Made you Stronger

THE DIFFERENCE

People can do you so dirty...
You probably wouldn't recognize
the difference between A Blessing
and what you're Use TO...

THE ENCOUNTER

She thought he was handsome
He thought she was sexy
She wanted to date him
He wanted to bed She
She wanted to get to know him
He wanted to get together
She was independent
He was self-sufficient and only thinking
Thinking with his little head for a certain reason
He had a hidden agenda
He was only there to commit treason
She was thinking long term
He was thinking more like seasons
You know from time to time to keep it convenient
She had a plan, but she knew she had to be smart
But what happened to her
she started thinking with her heart
They spent years back and forth
And yet she still didn't get the message
That he wasn't for her until she moved away and had to separate
the situation.

THE RING

Feb 14th
My last result
As I prayed to the Heavens...
Please let this work
Please can I save he
I hope he loves me
We can make this work
I brought two dozen of Roses
Reese's cup candy, Some candles
Some Lingerie & Skin
Some dim light and the Ring Draped in rose petals
With a card pouring out my deep instrumental
Waiting for the reaction as he walked through the door
My body trembled
We engaged in what I thought was a strong bond
But what I had gotten was the opposite
How he needs to think about it and didn't know I'd be sleeping alone.
That the next day through text he said...
I'm not Ready, I can't Accept IT... I don't want to hurt You

2 years later...
Another baby on the way!
I'm sorry I still Love YOU

THE SAME

I brought all these gifts
I paid for all these things
I hung in there when you had nothing
I spread my wings to fly
And yet I crashed again
I feel like I keep meeting the same guy
In another man's skin
It could just be my taste or a pretty bad habit
I feel like I got in the car after a drink, and had an awfully bad accident
Every time I think it may be different it ends up the same
I'm left holding this bag, and no one will save me

THE WAY

The way you use to look at me
The way you'd say my name
The way you ran your fingers through my hair
The way you held me close in the rain
Made me feel on top of the world
Like no one could ever take this feeling from me
Like you would always be with me
Like no one could break this bond we had
Like even if I were sad it would all disappear
yet despite my fears...
Something came... Approaching... Within A second...
Gone like a whirlwind
This relationship, my heart was then broken
You said, you'd never leave and I'm left trembling
Like a Thief in the night, stolen my prize possessions
Now I'm left with this constant pain...
Fury...
The depth of replayed memories and the deception...

THINGS NOT BEING SAID

I want you to be this guy
I want you to date me
I want you to bait me
I know we didn't start off in this direction
yet something has come over me
Besides the physical attraction
And the occasional sleepovers
I want more from you and I do adore you
I watch you sleep sometimes, and you hold my hand
Could it be... you want the same things
But you aren't ready to commit
They say you work for what you want
You pray for what you need
I just wonder is all in my head...

Or is it really things not being said

THINGS

Things to be Thankful for...
LIFE...LOVE...PEACE...AND
     HEALTH...

What's for you will be do not
     ENVY others...

You do not KNOW what
They had to do... To get where
     They Are

TIME

I GOT TIRED OF WASTING TIME
 AND STARTED MAKING TIME
BECAUSE I REALIZED I WAS RUNNING OUT OF TIME

TRUTH TO THE MATTER

I thought I knew what I was doing

But I made a mistake
But I didn't even see a smile upon my face
I feel a little hurt, discomfort, and some denial
Damn this might last for a little while
Maybe my destiny to be the one to see
That things as usual aren't meant to be
This year has brought much heartache and tears to my eyes, but the pain I seem to hide
And just seem to divide...
Who am I to take for granted, from those that want instead of need
I just thought he would finally see she.
No pressure, No Pushing, just a little triumph to gain
But I was a fool because then came the rain.
Falling upon my head, and then I'm left to endeavor my shame
And believe me at this point I'm more than sane

I kept trying to understand this shit is over
And all that was left awake was dew
But the one thing that plagues my mind
Is why you couldn't tell me the truth
You made me believe that friendship was alive and kicking
When you basically sent me to hell praying
To heaven to help my heart stop breaking
Death to the Silence has rose to the Midnight cry

Because the way I felt for you would be with me the rest of my life

Every day I wake up I put something passed me...
That the last time I gave myself to you...
Would be the last time you would ask me.

UNDONE

I owe you nothing still I explain myself to you
I still care for you and I want you in my life
But you are with someone else...
You tell me you still love me and if things were different.
But then would I be that one in the same predicament.
You say we met at the wrong time
I just think it was bullshit

UNSENT LETTER

I love you and you are going to be who you are. I can't change it. You have my heart and I don't know if you are aware of this. I don't even know why I bother explaining. I believe you know this, and I know I left but I'm selfish I want you to myself. And it won't happen but I'm just being honest. My mind tells me to leave you alone, but my heart still beats for you. You tell me you need me, but you've moved on to someone new. I knew it would happen eventually, but just thought we had something great. Men are greedy and they must have it all. I just was wondering if any of those things you said to me in the text last month were true? You make me fall in love with you all over again, but could we ever trust each other? Hmm could it ever be true?

UNTITLED 2

The heart of A man is worth everything
That he gives and he takes but he is breakable
In every means...

That he would never be emasculated
But he'll be broken
That sometimes he can understand what you are trying to say
But he will do what he wants to do any way
That no matter what, we'll somehow... try to make sense

Of what's the reason why we can't fix this failing relationship

UNTITLED

As I look into your eyes
It brings joy upon me
To breathe your air is a blessing
To hear your voice is music to my ears
If one day we could finish each other's sentences would be like
Deja vu
To make love would be like a symphony
The bass from the orchestra is like the thumping of a heartbeat
I would want you lying next to me night after night
Just to be in the arms of someone that really loves you
They say if you seek you shall find
But when I met You, I wasn't really looking
Just if you were coal and were rubbed into a beautiful diamond
Like a cold night lit by a fire
I'd throw lighter fluid, so you'd never burn out
You're my moth to my flame
A part of my soul that has no name
My favorite song I'd keep on repeat
I think you are the person in my dreams
But you have not yet appeared before me
I've pictured you to be imperfect, but in a clear view
I wish you knew what's in my thoughts how I could spend every
moment with you
This could be quite endearing as I can feel your lips nearing
My mind is steering me into all types of directions
We've formed this deep connection
And it tears me apart, that we're separated.

USING

People use people now a days
They don't use things
No one knows about being genuine
They know about handling you
Telling you what they think you want to hear
Being manipulative and changing faces
Trying to exploit your darkest secrets
Massaging your ego to the max
Trying not to go too far
But just enough to the limit
Enough to know when to pull back
Using enough to hope you never snap

VIBE

I met you
I liked our conversation
I called we vibed a little
We linked up
We drank a bit and exchanged thoughts
I admired you and you sought me out
As we continued your vibe spoke to me
Not that I wanted to spend my life with you
But I really want you to get to know me

WALKING

If you can't FIGURE Out where you Stand
With Someone...
Then IT's Time TO START WALKING...

WEARY

My pain is of weary
My pain is of shame
That if only a few will speak my name in vain
That my thoughts will one day kill me
That through me of love I was taught
That the houses I have visited no more offer comfort
That many will see her as what she could have been
That she fought many of battles and to this day I recommend
Show those you care and much of support
Of many of depression, and many of quiet nights we have fought.
That even though she rests of many nights
There has not been any peace.
That one day she will love me
As we share the thoughts of triumph and Melancholy.

WHAT I WANT

Even though you can't give me what I want
Why do you come back to me?
Why do you condition me with the nonsense...
Why do you make it sound so easy,
when in fact it's heartbreaking to the core.
You keep me yearning for more
I try to stay away, but you found a way to make it work.
Then we're back to the same shit again...
And you become this Game Changer...
You Stole my inner peace
My soul is somewhere lingering
Just to her your voice, just to see your smile
Just to hear your breathing
Just wanting you here beside me,
next to me
Invading my space.
Just wanting you to need me.
Yet at again time has passed
I let you in and 2 months it last
Then I realize I have to grab my keys,
unlock the door, and Start the ignition
Run away from you because I'm the fool
This will never be a Relationship...

WHEN WINDOWS BLOW

You were my light but left me in darkness
My sighs were cries and nothing matters
My deep breathes became faints and sighs become wanders
Then I reminisce on the love we made
Shadows appear thick and I clinch my pillow
As my tears shed and wilt like rose petals
Apart of me is gone again I have to face
The break of dawn and sun shining
Heartfelt banter I once proclaimed
Sometimes I wish I never knew your name
The words I speak are unfamiliar to me
The moments we'd shared just pillow talk once we would speak
Pain is endeavored as I pass my hand upon these sheets as you are
no longer my man
A mere thought that shall pass accordingly
My future I once grasped that longs to let me weep
The one person I'd long to feel beside me
Inside of me
To straddle your waist.
The warmth I'd taste, just has wasted away from me
Who are you to me
My soul had been ripped from inside of me
The one I felt could vary with the challenges I seek to bare
The man I love hath love for not me but some other feminine
The touch of his hand that made my body quiver
The love I thought we made have only my rhythm

When I gyrated my hips to always become as one
I seek to find but the one I'm looking for
Has taken with him. No matter if he thinks not as such
At the end of the day my love has become
Lost in this mythology
Cause the goddess of love lies inside of me
That giving You sometimes gave me
That I expected You to be a part of she
That no matter what I want to take thee upon my breast
Stroke your ego with positive thoughts till there's nothing left
Cause that part of the Rib that Adam gave Eve
Made me feel you were a part of me
Somehow some way you've taken a Toll on Me
You gave me sobriety when moments were dim
And you didn't know at the time what you were dealing with
We shared something so kind
I wish you were mine, but u choose to be else where
No longer you want her to stare
But to walk this world alone
To not acknowledge your tarry
When at the end if You I'd had to carry would be my Equal or to be
most to a par
You were everything I thought I was looking for
A message in a bottle I have sent
Indulge in intimacy for I have bargained
A woman you have bedded not once as a child
My heart was open when I met you
Once you captivated me with your Smile.... The worlds collide
when we met in Harmony
Once you sighted to not choose me over sensitivity...

WORRY

He said to me I've been hurt before
I said me too
He said he only deals with one at a time
I said let's see
He told me these things
And now I worry
I worry it isn't just me
I want to trust these things
But can I see passed the many men that have said the same to me?

Told me it was only You
And I don't want anybody... else
It's just so hard to not know
Or draw negative attention to yourself
I don't worry about other women
I worry about the hurt
I worry about being alone
I worry about not having you to myself
I worry that I may come on too strong
I worry that this maybe the end
I worry in these cases and there are plenty of men
But what you don't know
It's only one you

Nobody makes me feel the way you do
The way you look at me
Make me feel like I'm the only one in the room
When you said what you said in the beginning
It Was like you wanted loyalty and truth

I wanted to give it to you that day forth
Make a believer out of me
Please tell me you didn't lie to me
Please tell me you aren't apart of the cult
The culture of men that play games with women's hearts.
Please be different
I don't want to keep suffering
From what some other woman did to you and giving you another man's punishment.

WROTE IT BECAUSE
I KNOW IT

How do you breathe without the one you love
How do you hold on to your heart with pain
How do you cry sometimes not knowing comfort
You try to do it with ease
Because we all try to understand why certain things can't be
I cared enough to give you me
You took my feelings and chose to demean me
you betrayed my trust and left me
I hold you responsible and in contempt
I didn't force love upon you
You made a decision
Now I'm left in a lonely place
What saddens me is the love that can't be replaced
How many times can you hurt and not acknowledge the good
How was I there and you didn't appreciate it
How Do I Love Again
We do eventually take time out to see
What's the becoming of me
I take my life seriously
Play close attention to the ones around you
They can either stay or tear what you made a disaster
Sometimes we replace pain with hours of work
We disguise our troubled moments with money and say we're
proud of it
Longing for that attachment that may have been Bliss
These are the things I tend to miss

I love hard sometimes without the intent
Unnoticed situations, that take a toll later down the road
And I haven't wrote this way before
You say
I stole your heart... But u stole my joy
When you chose not only to walk out the door
But you left me unknowing
Maybe I think you're beneath my thoughts of what I wanted to exceed
I gave much pleasure in everything I sort out to win
But Men Walk Away Faster Than Women...
And Later That's What We are Left to Deal With

YOUR CALLING

Sometimes you just have to realize some things, and people aren't for you. Move on to know that eventually something better will pique your interest and inspire
What's inside!!
Realize your calling.

ABOUT THE AUTHOR

Keshia L. Williams

Hello my name is Keshia L. Williams and I'm writing you to discuss my poetry. I have a love for the arts, music, people, and self expression. I moved from Newark, NJ to Atlanta, GA, to start the next chapter of life, moments, and inner peace.

My direction I want to go in is to discuss love, relationships, and raw feelings. My book Journey Of a Poet is who I am, and what I have experienced in my life as a child, adolescent, just as well as coming into adulthood.

I've been writing since I was 7, and had a wise soul beyond my years since I was 8. I was given the opportunity to write children's books, as a child, but was told I needed to enjoy my childhood in which I was stripped from unknowingly.

I have a voice and I want to share that with others to know spoken word is for the healing. It's ok to release your past and speak out.

I wanted to be a psychologist, but I really realized later cognitive behavioral therapy is the way... just as well as life coaching. I want to give a person the opportunity to live out loud, live in their truth, and not be ashamed of who they are because strength is the key to excellence.

Made in the USA
Columbia, SC
24 August 2020

17341459R00064